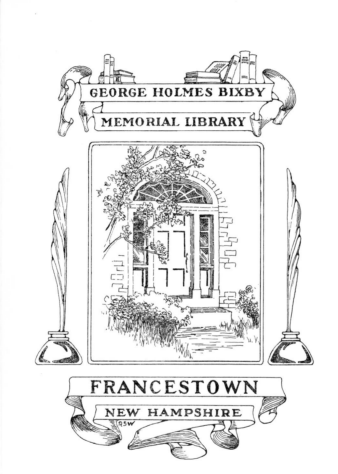

IN MEMORY OF LIBRARY TRUSTEE
JUDY DANFORTH
2003

Light

The Scribbles Institute™ Young Artist Basics

Published by The Child's World®
PO Box 326
Chanhassen, MN 55317-0326
800-599-READ
www.childsworld.com

Design and Production: The Creative Spark, San Juan Capistrano, CA
Series Editor: Elizabeth Sirimarco Budd

Photos:
© Fine Art Photographic Library, London/Art Resource, NY: cover
© Alinari/Art Resource, NY: 10, 12, 27
© Corel Corporation: 22, 23
© Erich Lessing/Art Resource, NY: 15, 30
© Fine Art Photographic Library, London/Art Resource, NY: 24
© Giraudon/Art Resource, NY: 9; 21
© Jet Propulsion Laboratory, California Institute of Technology: 16
© PhotoDisc: 28, 29
© Michael S. Yamashita/CORBIS: 18

Library of Congress Cataloging-in-Publication Data
Court, Robert, 1956–
  Light / by Rob Court.
       p. cm. — (Young artists basics series)
Includes index.
Summary: Presents examples of the use of light and shadow in various
objects of art throughout history.
  ISBN 1-56766-080-0 (alk. paper)
 1. Light in art—Juvenile literature. 2. Shades and shadows in
art—Juvenile literature. 3. Painting—Technique—Juvenile literature.
4. Art appreciation—Juvenile literature. [1. Light in art. 2. Shadows.
3. Art appreciation.] I. Title. II. Series.
  ND1484 .C68 2002
  701'.8—dc21
                                    2002005554

Light

Rob Court

The Child's World

Loopi is a line,
a fantastic line.

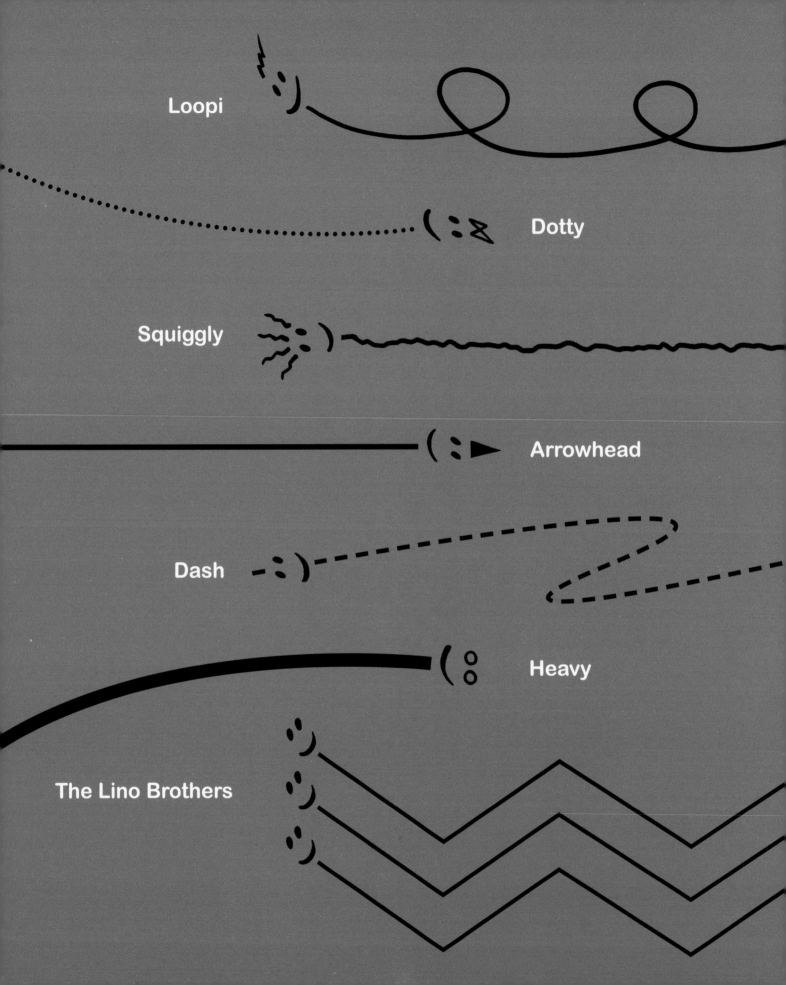

Loopi

Dotty

Squiggly

Arrowhead

Dash

Heavy

The Lino Brothers

There are many kinds of lines.

Some are dotted lines.

Some are squiggly lines.

Some lines point in a direction.

Some lines are drawn with dashes.

Other lines are very, very thick.

Sometimes lines work together
to help you understand light.

For thousands of years, light has helped people see beautiful things. Egyptian artisans made the **columns** in this picture more than 2,200 years ago. Light and shadow help you see the columns' form.

Look at the picture. Can you find Dotty? She shows you the side of a column where the sun is shining. The light is bright.

Loopi shows you another side of the same column. Here less sunlight shines. This side has a shadow.

Dash shows you the column's shadow on the ground. There is less sunlight here, too. Shadows look smaller when they are farther away.

Artists in ancient Greece created this stone **sculpture.** Light helps you see the form of the man's face. Light shines on areas that look bright. Where less light shines, you see shadows.

This Greek sculpture is more than 2,000 years old. Can you find Dotty in the picture? She helps you see light and shadow. Can you see bright areas where there is more light? Can you see dark areas where there is less light? Study the rest of the picture. Can you find different shadows?

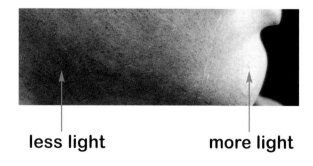

less light   more light

The artist Michelangelo made this drawing more than 500 years ago. Learning about light and shadows was important to him.

Michelangelo's drawing was created on paper. He started this picture of a woman by drawing an **outline.** Then he drew shadows where less light would shine on a person's face.

Can you find Dotty in Michelangelo's artwork? She helps you see an outline. Can you see other lines in the drawing? Can you see the shadows on the woman's face?

Left: Michelangelo, *Head of a Young Woman,* **date unknown. Graphite on paper.**

For hundreds of years, artists and scientists have studied light. At right is a painting by Jan Vermeer. The sun shines through the window. Outside the room, the light is bright. The space inside has many shadows.

Look for Arrowhead in Vermeer's painting. He helps you see how light shines through the window. Things that are farther away from the window are darker. Can you find the brightest areas of the room? Can you find the darkest shadows?

Right: Jan Vermeer, *The Astronomer,* 1668. Oil on canvas.

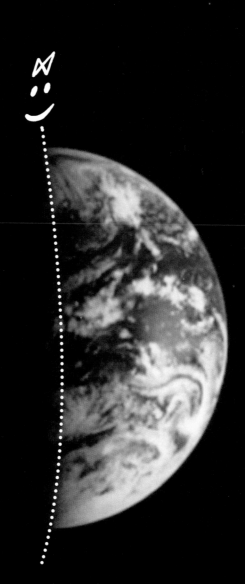

Planet Earth is round. Its form is a **sphere.** The moon is a smaller sphere. Around the earth and moon, the space is black. Do you see the colors where the sun shines on the spheres? Where less light hits the spheres, the colors become darker.

Dotty shows you where earth's form curves away from the light. Where the light does not shine, there is shadow. Can you see where the shadow begins on the moon's form? Are the moon's colors different from the earth's?

The place where light comes from is called the light source. The sun is a light source. It is shining on top of this sculpture. The large, red form in this picture is a **cube.** It is standing on its corner!

Right: Arrowhead shows how the light source in the picture shines on the cube. The light shines from above. The side facing the light is red. The sides that face away from the light source are darker red.

Study the picture at left. Which sides of the cube are darker? Can you see the shadow on the ground?

light source

shadow

In this painting by Claude Monet, the light source is the sun. Arrowhead shows you where the sunlight is coming from.

The right side of the woman's dress is bright. The left side of her dress is in the shade. There is a dark shadow on the ground.

Can you see how the woman's white dress changes in the shade? What other colors do you see on the dress?

Right: Claude Monet, *Woman with Umbrella,* 1886. Oil on canvas.

Light helps you see the bright and dark colors of things in nature.

Below is a picture of a leopard resting under a tree. The leopard's body is in the shade. Colors are darker in the shade. Can you see areas where the sun is shining on the leopard's face? Colors are brighter when they are not shaded.

Can you find Dash in the picture above? He helps you see the shaded areas of a rose. Look for other dark and light shades of red in the picture.

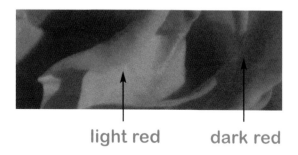

light red   dark red

23

The candle in this picture is bright. The light on the woman's face is bright, too. Where there is less light, the colors are darker. Shadows and light help you see the forms of people and things.

This painting by Petrus van Schendel shows a candle near the center. It is a light source. Do you see other light sources in the painting?

Can you find Dotty in the painting? She shows you shadows and dark colors. The point where the brightest light shines on something is called a highlight.

shadow

highlight

Left: Petrus van Schendel, *Market Stall,* **date unknown. Oil on canvas.**

25

The white snow creates many highlights in this painting by Ricardo Ferrara. The car is dark with bright snow on top of it. Can you see other dark areas that are close to bright areas?

Colors look lighter when they are far away. How are the faraway buildings different from the buildings that are closer?

Right: Ricardo Ferrara, *Snowing Via Vittorio Veneto,* 1929. Oil on canvas.

Find Dash in the painting. He shows a man with an umbrella. How are the colors of the man's clothes different from the woman's dress on page 21? Are the shadows on the ground different in the two paintings?

When light shines on metal, you can see bright highlights.

Can you see the brightest highlights on the metal **cylinders** below?
Can you see the color blue on the cylinders?

Sometimes you cannot see bright highlights on metal.

Can you find Dotty in both pictures? She shows you different kinds of highlights and shadows. How does the light shine differently on the cylinders?

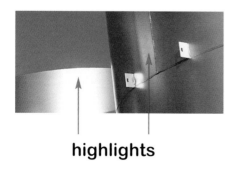

highlights

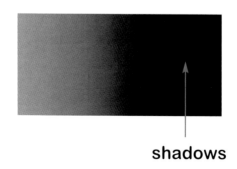

shadows

Paul Cezanne, *Pots, Bottle, Cup, and Fruit,* 1871. Oil on canvas.

Light is very important in this **still life** painted by Paul Cezanne. Can you guess where the light comes from? Can you guess what kind of light source is shining on these things? Is it the sun? A lamp? A candle?

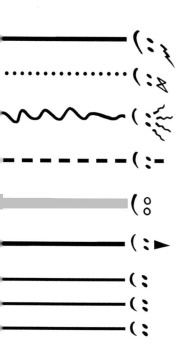

Put It All Together

Take a minute to study the painting by Cezanne. He used many different colors in his artwork. Can you find the bright colors? Can you find the dark colors? Can you find highlights in the painting? Do you see areas where light and shadows help you see things?

Create Your Own Still Life

You can use ideas from Cezanne's still life for your own painting. Use the sun or a lamp for a light source. Shadows help you see the form of things on a table. Sit far enough away to see everything on the table. Start by drawing outlines. Look for light and shadow as you paint or draw the things in your still life.

Students, Teachers, and Parents

LOOPI the Fantastic Line™ is always waiting to help you learn more about drawing and light—at www.scribblesinstitute.com. You can get helpful ideas for your drawings at the Scribbles Institute™. It's a great place for students, teachers, and parents to find books, information, and tips about drawing. You can even get advice from a drawing coach!

The Scribbles Institute™

SCRIBBLESINSTITUTE.COM

Glossary

columns (KOL-ums)
Columns are tall, slender structures used to support or decorate a building. Columns can be made of stone, wood, metal, or other materials.

cube (KYOOB)
A cube is a solid object with six square sides. Dice in a board game are cubes.

cylinders (SILL-in-derz)
Cylinders are hollow or solid objects shaped like round poles or tubes. A tin can is a cylinder.

outline (OWT-line)
An outline is a line that shows the shape of an object. A drawing done in outlines shows only an object's outer lines.

sculpture (SKULP-cher)
A sculpture is a work of art formed into a shape to represent something. Sculptures can be carved from stone or made from metal.

sphere (SFEER)
A sphere is a round, solid object. A ball is an example of a sphere.

still life (STILL LIFE)
A still life is a picture that shows nonliving things. A still life might show a bowl of fruit, for example.

Index

About the Author
Rob Court is a designer and illustrator. He has a studio in San Juan Capistrano, California. He started the Scribbles Institute™ to help people learn about the importance of drawing and creativity.

This book is dedicated to Jesse and Jasmine.

701   Court, Rob.
COU
          Light.

$27.79

DATE		
AUG 0 6 2003		
NOV 1 8 2003		
MAY 1 1 2004		
DISCARD		

0403

GEORGE HOLMES BIXBY MEM LIB
FRANCESTOWN NH

BAKER & TAYLOR